The Easy Yes

No more maybes – how to attract coaching clients who are ready to say yes

Janine Coombes

Do It On Purpose Publishing

First published in 2025 © Janine Coombes and Do It On Purpose Publishing

Cover image and illustrations: Reb Capper, Steamboat Creative

Typesetting and proofreading: Vicky Quinn-Fraser

Editor: Amy Warren

ISBN13 Paperback: 978-1-0685827-0-7

ISBN Ebook: 978-1-0685827-1-4

www.janinecoombes.co.uk

Contents

Foreword 1

I've known Janine for over five years, back when she was a member of my content marketing membership community. Every week, my job was to critique her content... and every week, I'd almost forget to critique her actual work because I was too damn busy learning from it.

Janine has this rare ability to explain complex business concepts simply, without dumbing them down. She's sharp, strategic, and a genuinely lovely and funny person — and this book is full of her magic.

One of the things I love most about this book is how clearly it pinpoints why coaches struggle with marketing.

The majority of coaches are hardwired to help. But the problem is that many coaches are pouring time and energy into people who don't yet realise they need help. They don't have the right budget to invest, or their mindset isn't quite ready for coaching.

This book helps you stop trying to convince the unconvinceable and start focusing on the people who are ready to take action.

Janine shows you how to speak to the people who are ready for transformation. This book won't just help you sell more. It will help you sell to the right people: the ones who value your work, get incredible results, and make you fall in love with your business all over again.

Lyndsay Cambridge, co-author of Content Fortress and co-founder of Jammy

Foreword 2

I entered the online marketing world in 2003 and for over 15 years, marketing felt like climbing Everest in flip flops. No matter how much effort I put in, it felt slow, exhausting, and it rarely led to results that matched my efforts. I was following advice from online "gurus" and it wasn't working for me. But instead of questioning the strategies I was being taught, I blamed myself.

Every sales page started with defining the problem, convincing people they needed to take action and then showing them how my work could be the answer. It was exhausting for clients and for me. And it didn't work.

In *The Easy Yes*, Janine describes this as the "Dead Zone": we, the coach-shaped people, can see a person has got a problem and needs to do something about it, but they can't yet. That's where I put most of my marketing effort for over a decade, and I wondered why it was such hard work.

That shift to finding our audience's sweet spot changes everything. Now, rather than spending time trying to educate those who have no idea that Imposter Syndrome even exists, I focus on connecting with people who already know how much it is holding them or their teams back and are looking for a proven way forward. It's such a relief for them and for me. And it works.

If marketing feels like hard work and isn't bringing the results your efforts deserve, read *The Easy Yes*. It's practical, no-nonsense, totally non-judgemental, and you can finish it in one sitting... but bringing Janine's strategies into your marketing could help you to change the world.

Clare Josa, Author of Ditching Imposter Syndrome

Introduction

Have you ever had a wonderful sales call with a prospective client only for them to change their mind with no real explanation? Or created a bunch of content like posting on LinkedIn, writing blog posts or recording podcasts only to realise you're getting more clients through word of mouth? Or has a keen-sounding client kept you hanging for months even though you know they sorely need your services?

If you nodded yes to any of those things, then you're not alone. I've been there, done that. Let me take you back... I started my business following a ten year career in corporate marketing. I decided to go it alone once I'd had kids so I didn't have to do the two-and-a-half hour round trip commute into London every day. I remember thinking the easiest bit of running my own business would be the marketing, since I've got so much training and experience in it.

HA! What a joke!

I now realise that, when it comes to marketing and selling your own stuff, it's multitudes more difficult. Especially if you're working with your clients in a high-touch way. It feels like you're selling... you. All the mindset monkeys come out to play when you're trying to tell people you're good at something and can actually help them.

Very slowly, I came to. And I finally started applying my marketing knowledge to my own business. I went back to basics and got clear on who I wanted to work with, why they'd want to work with me, and what they were actually looking for. I put my first offer out there and the rest is history!

When I start working with clients, these are the types of things they're struggling with too. They're spending a lot of time marketing with not enough to show for it.

If you're picking up this book, you're probably out to make a positive change in the world rather than a quick buck. You started coaching to help people in some way and not to spend your days marketing and selling.

Why have I written this book for coach-shaped-people in particular? Coaching was the key that unlocked the "real Janine." I lost myself in my teens and twenties; as many people do. I didn't even realise I was creative for a couple of decades! I'm now in the privileged position of having been coached by all sorts of coaches. The result? I feel like the Janine I was in primary school. When I felt like I could take on the world and being me was just the best thing ever.

I went from lost and lacking self-awareness to the leader of my own personal mission, learning to trust my gut more and more every day. Being coached was the road back to being me again. And that's why I love working with coaches the absolute most, because I know if you could wave a magic wand and help everyone in the whole world all at the same time, you'd be waggling that stick like crazy!

I also understand the paradox of trying to run a business when you're a good-hearted coach-shaped-person. People need to be ready for coaching before they buy, so you don't want to be pushy. But you know you need to get the word out there that you can help people. But you don't want to be spammy and salesy. And round and round the merry-go-round goes!

This book invites you to step off a while.

Let's stand back and get some perspective. And while you're there, have a gander at a nifty tool I devised to help my clients work out where to focus their efforts.

I wrote this book for you and all other coach-shaped-people who are tearing their hair out due to marketing. It feels like you need to do *more* marketing to help more people. You don't. You just need to know which marketing to do and how.

Using the Easy Yes model, you'll be able to:

- See why some clients seem keen to work with you but then trot off to work with a different coach.
- Spot the gaps in your marketing you can then fill and make easier sales, ethically.
- Reduce the amount of effort you're putting into sales and marketing while getting better results.

I know, I know, this whole "having to do sales and marketing" can be pretty tedious. It's not what you signed up for when you set up your coaching business, was it? You just want to crack on and help as many people as possible!

But you can only do that if the right people know who you are and that you're the right person for them.

As a wise person once said, "To do the work you love, you need to win the work you love." And that's what this book is all about — making it as easy as possible for the right people to say a resounding YES to what you have to offer.

Most sales and marketing conundrums can be solved by knowing the prospective client better. What do *they* think they need? Do they even believe what you do can help them? Do they agree *you're* the right person to help them? The answer lies in how you're positioning what you do in the eyes of the people you'd love to work with. It's usually a mix of all these things that add up to why someone buys and why someone else won't. It's that combination that'll unlock an "Easy Yes" from people. That's what we're going to cover.

The Easy Yes model combines different strands of buyer behaviour and puts you back in the driver's seat, so you can see what's going on; why some things are working and why some things aren't.

And more importantly, arm you with the clarity you need to streamline your marketing efforts so you'll be able to get the easiest yeses of your business so far without running yourself ragged trying to get clients.

Are you ready? Let's dive in!

Chapter 1
Why do people buy?

The Easy Yes model is built on two things; why would someone buy *now* and why would they buy from *you*. Let's start with why they'd buy now.

There's so much research and a multitude of books about buyer psychology and the buyer decision making journey. Or to put it another way, "sales funnel."

Cue strangled scream

Either way, people are dying to know why people buy so they can encourage them to do more of it!

Whenever I speak to clients about the thoughts and feelings their clients will be going through before making a decision about whether to buy coaching, there's one buyer journey that makes the most sense for coaching services. Let me tell you about it...

My favourite buyer journey

It's hilarious that most models illustrating the steps someone takes towards making a buying decision focus on the *brand* (or in other words the seller), not the person buying the stuff. What's that all about?

Kenda MacDonald shared her interpretation of a buyer decision-making process in her 2019 book *Hack the Buyer Brain*. I love it for two reasons:

1. It's client-focused. This is essential! Getting to know your clients and how self-aware they are is so important when buying something high-investment like coaching.
2. It just makes sense!

Below is my simplified version, where I've changed the wording from "problem awareness" to "desire awareness." This is because people get coaching because they want to move towards a certain outcome or away from something painful or unpleasant (or both), not necessarily to solve a "problem."

Therefore, I've called it the Desire Awareness Journey because it's all about the buyer gradually going through the process of understanding what they want and need. They can "desire" to solve a problem or they can "desire" to make a change in their life or business. It's more accurate to talk in these terms when it comes to coaching services.

The Desire Awareness Journey

1. Desire unaware
V
2. Desire aware, solution unaware (research phase)
V
3. Desire and solution aware (research phase)
V
4. Decision time

1. Desire unaware

It all kicks off with a potential client who doesn't realise they want to change anything yet. Not the kind of transformation you're offering to address, anyway. At this point there is no chance whatsoever that they'll buy your service.

An example of this stage of the journey is when there's someone you'd love to help, but they are as yet unaware of what is possible *for them.* For example, 'That's okay for so-and-so, they're extroverted. I could never speak on a stage."

Coaching is rarely, if ever, an impulse purchase. It's bought because the client thinks they need it. They will not buy unless they want a result they believe coaching could help them with, or have a situation they think coaching could help them move away from. And they need to believe the outcomes are realistic for them.

2. Desire aware (but solution unaware)

The potential coachee realises something's up. They start to learn more about their situation and do some research. During research, they might put a label on their problem or aspiration, such as, "Oh, I'm self-sabotaging!" or "I wish I could feel more fulfilled in my work."

3. Desire aware and solution aware

They've asked around, they've noodled online, and they've got some options. But they don't know which solution to pick. They're in "whittle down" mode.

4. Decision time

The client has become so excited about one of the options, or so in need to fix their situation, they want to make a decision NOW. At this point they take some action, which we'd hope would be to work with you!

How long does the Desire Awareness Journey take? Bearing in mind that humans are fickle beasts, each stage could take hours, days, or even years! Sometimes they can move backwards and forwards and not move in a handy linear way like we'd want them to:

How we want people to make decisions

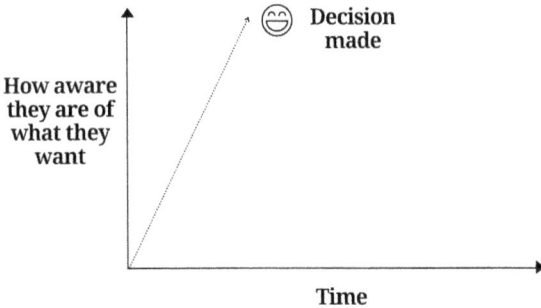

However, important purchase decisions usually happen a bit more like this:

How people usually make decisions

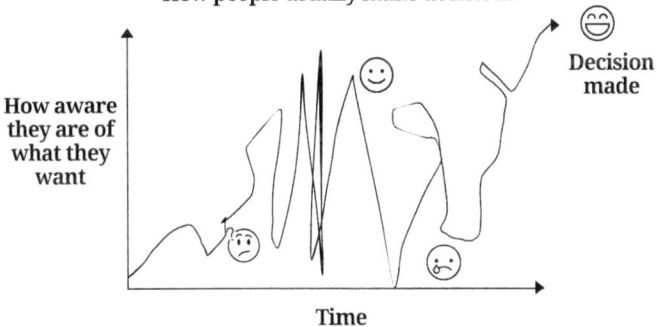

But fear not! We're going to clarify why some of those seemingly erratic peaks and troughs happen, and how to handle them, later on in the book. And, just to keep things spicy, we can stir Trigger Events into the mix too...

Chapter 1 Summary: What was that all about then?

Before a client will buy anything, they'll want something to change in their lives. They'll either want to move away from something unpleasant, move towards something desirable, or both. But before they take action, they need to be aware of that desire for change and what solutions are available to them. And finally, when they have enough info, they'll feel confident to make a decision about whether to buy something or not.

Your turn

Pick one of your clients. What steps of awareness did they go through before making the decision to buy from you?

Here's an example for a client of a productivity coach who works with ideas people who have trouble following through with implementation:

Desire unaware	Client thinks they are the problem. They're not good enough or they're incapable of getting things done.
Desire aware, solution unaware (research phase)	Client sees other people seeming to be able to finish multiple projects with ease. They start reading up about productivity and try a planner or two.
Desire and solution aware (research phase)	Client is fed up with planners that don't help and prescriptive advice that doesn't work. They become aware of mentors and coaches as an option.
Decision time	Client decides a productivity coach is the right choice for them. Books a call to discuss.

As you'll know from the introduction of this book — being coached changed my life. The example above tracks the journey I went on that led me to work with my amazing productivity coach.

I know how powerful coaching is, which is why I want to help wonderful coach-shaped-people have a bigger impact in the world!

Fill your client's journey out in this table:

The Easy Yes

Desire unaware	
Desire aware, solution unaware (research phase)	
Desire and solution aware (research phase)	
Decision time	

Or download the companion worksheets at:

janinecoombes.co.uk/yes-resources

Chapter 2
Trigger events

Jogging alongside the Desire Awareness Journey, ready to pop their heads up at any moment, are trigger events. These are things that happen in a person's life that suddenly make them aware of a new piece of knowledge or prod them to take action NOW.

Triggers are sometimes listed as part of a buyer decision-making process, but in reality they don't appear at the same stage of the process for everyone. Again, humans are messy. Instead, triggers just crop up at some random time, like one of those calls during the middle of your dinner to ask you if you've been in an accident and "did you know you could sue someone?"

However unpredictable they are, they're rather handy because a trigger acts as a catalyst to the next stage of the Desire Awareness Journey. A trigger event can even whisk the voyager straight to decision time.

When trigger events happen, they can:

- Make the buyer aware that they want a change (they become desire aware) e.g. a parent assumes everyone gets so frustrated with their kids that they shout at them, until they see their friends managing mornings calmly, so they seek a parenting coach (this was me when my kids were toddlers!)
- Make them aware of a solution (they become solution aware) e.g. a 48-year-old woman assumes everyone at that age feels knackered all the time, but then they see a video from a menopause coach explaining how they could be feeling. (Again, me!)
- Force someone's hand and mean they skip on to decision time before doing any research at all, as in the story below.

Here's an example of a real live human going through the Desire Awareness Journey. This is a story of one of my client's clients. Let's call her Beth.

Beth was a high-achieving, high-powered executive. She thrived on people telling her she was doing a good job and had steadily and swiftly been promoted. By the age of 40 she was on the board of directors at a large multinational. She was often stressed, missing out on family life and friends, but she thought that was how work was meant to be so she doubled down and carried on. Beth was desire unaware — she felt no need to change.

The pressure didn't let up. It compounded. "I just need to work harder! I know how to do that," she thought. That's when the insomnia and mild panic attacks started. She wasn't particularly worried, though. She had a nice holiday coming up and she thought that would do the trick. She wanted to take some action, but she didn't realise a holiday wasn't going to cut it. Beth was desire aware but solution unaware.

The holiday came and went in a blip. Naturally, all her work was waiting for her when she came back. And a whole lot more. One Saturday morning she collapsed in a supermarket and ended up in hospital unable to move. Beth had experienced a trigger event.

When she gained consciousness and got over the shock of waking up in hospital with a body that would no longer obey her commands, she started looking for solutions. She asked medical staff for advice, she searched for answers on the internet, and she confided in friends. She created a shortlist of things she could try to reverse her condition and prevent it from happening again. Beth was desire aware and solution aware.

And, finally, she decided to work with a burnout coach. Beth had arrived at decision time.

How to use triggers in your marketing

The various triggers a potential client might go through are precious golden nuggets you can use in a variety of ways to connect with your best fit clients and show them it's time to take action, *before* something drastic happens. Most coaches I know don't want their clients to experience a catastrophic event before they make a change! They want to help them avoid that.

But humans be humaning. They tend to keep plodding on, deceiving themselves that things aren't really that bad and perhaps it will magically change without having to take any action.

The tricky thing is that your prospective client might well notice something's awry, but several things are likely:

- They may see it as just a little niggle and not something they need to take immediate action on.
- They might think they can deal with it themselves or *should* be able to handle it themselves (as is often the case with high-achievers.)
- They might take a small action (akin to sticking a plaster on a festering wound) like taking a supplement. This gives them the feeling of doing something useful but in reality it's delaying them getting a full resolution.

The fact that good coaching is rarely cheap and requires a leap of faith to participate in means it's oh-so-easy for people to muddle around with half-fixes for years without taking action on the change they want to make deep down.

This is one of the most frustrating things about being a coach, isn't it? You want to help people *before* they get desperate. You want to save them from heartache and stress. You want to change their life *now* not in five years' time when they're huddled and quivering in a dark corner.

But it's much easier to sell a cure than a prevention. For instance, it's hard to convince people with insomnia to eat better, get more fresh air, and reduce their stress levels. It's much easier to sell them a snazzy disposable heated eye mask.

And in our example above, it was only because Beth had a massive life-pausing event that she *had* to take some immediate action. Fate forced her hand. She became acutely "desire aware" and scrambled to become "solution aware" as quickly as possible. Trying to sell her something six months before would've been nigh on impossible.

I can sense you're probably exasperated and almost hear you exclaim, "Arghh, what's the point!" as I write this. But fear not, you can still try to engage people like Beth before it's too late. To do this, use symptoms instead.

Symptoms

Symptoms are like mini-triggers. You can mention them in your marketing as reasons to work with you before their situation gets too dire. Here are some examples:

- If you're a leadership coach, you could look out for companies who are planning a restructure since reorganising teams is a common trigger for buying a culture change programme.
- If you're a menopause coach, symptoms abound! For instance, your prospective client might be struggling with their relationship with their partner due to lack of sleep and irritability. You could ask if they've had a blow-out row that week. This example might work for a woman who tends not to take action for her own sake but might do it for the sake of an important relationship.
- If you're a career coach who helps people find new dream roles, you could call to people who've been

made redundant and who are dreading the thought of applying for jobs and doing interviews.
- If you're a health coach, you could explain their kids are likely to copy their non-existent self-care and follow suit with lack of exercise and poor nutrition.

A friend of mine, Amanda Webb, helps people with their Google analytics and has coined the phrase "analytics face" to describe the disgusted or confused expression people pull when they open their dashboard. She's put a name on a symptom and linked it to what she can do to help.

Not all symptoms will have the same level of impact. You might hit on one that absolutely nails it and it'll help you explain more clearly than ever why your perfect fit clients should work with you. But it's more likely you'll need to experiment with weaving in all relevant symptoms into your marketing messages and see which combination lands the best.

Trigger and symptom clusters

Sometimes there isn't a single trigger or symptom that makes people finally take the plunge. It's a combination of things all happening around the same time that prompts action. Or it could be a build-up that happens over months or even years until they reach the final straw.

For instance, I'd been thinking about writing a book for years. But the reason I finally took the plunge was a combination of a client asking me why I hadn't written a book yet, me running a workshop with material that felt much beefier than usual, and the book coach I'd been stalking sending me a LinkedIn message simply asking, "If not now, then when?" Yes, you messaging someone or them seeing your marketing could be a trigger to take action! But only if it matches what they want at that moment i.e. if they're desire *and* solution aware. We'll talk more about how to do that later on in the book.

***

Chapter 2 Summary: What was that all about then?

People are most likely to buy high-investment services like coaching when they're absolutely convinced they need it. This might be a gentle awakening following them noticing a series of "symptoms" or after a more major trigger or set of triggers.

Your turn

Think of a client you've loved working with in the last year or so — someone you'd love to clone if you could and work with more people like them.

Now fill in what they're likely to be seeing, hearing, doing or saying. See if you can uncover some symptoms or triggers you can mention in your marketing to help them self-diagnose. For example, if you were a leadership coach specialising in newly promoted managers it might look something like this:

Seeing	Other managers in the organisation seem to be doing it all effortlessly.
Hearing	Line manager saying that they need to be more authoritative or strategic.
Doing	Avoiding difficult conversations and conflict.
Saying	'Perhaps I'm not cut out for this.' 'Perhaps I should get another job.'

Now fill out what this ideal customer is immersed in every day. You might want to play with the point of view you're coming from, e.g. you could write it *as* your ideal client. "Today *I* heard someone say X that made *me* feel Y."

Seeing	
Hearing	
Doing	
Saying	

Don't want to scribble in the book? Download the printable companion worksheets at:

janinecoombes.co.uk/yes-resources

Chapter 3
Why would people buy from YOU?

O kay, so we've had a whistle stop tour of the thought processes people go through before making a decision to buy coaching or not. Now we get to the juicy stuff — why would they buy from *you*?

And, thus, I wheel out one of the oldest and cheesiest phrases in marketing:

Know. Like. Trust.

I've seen marketers vying for clicks online saying that good old "know like trust" is nonsense. Or that it's "dead."

eyeroll

Let's examine that shall we?

I don't particularly like Shell as an organisation. And I certainly don't trust them with our environment. But do I know them? Yes, I am aware of their existence. Do I like that when my car is about to run out of fuel, they're there on the side of the road for me to swing in and nip to the loo while

I'm at it? Yes. I like that. And do I trust that I'll be able to fill up my car with their product and it won't explode in a ball of flames? Yes. I trust their product to do the job I'm paying for.

Know, like and trust is alive and well.

IN YOUR FACE DAFT CLICKBAIT MARKETERS!

I know what you're thinking... "Well there was that thing I bought from a Facebook ad and I didn't know, like, and trust them. And there was that coach I worked with who I only knew because a friend told me about her..."

There are two exceptions that prove the rule:

1. Something cheap with low emotional risk means you're likely to be able to take a punt on it without that Know Like Trust thing in full swing. You feel safe giving it a try. If it turns out to be a bad choice, it won't affect you much.
2. And with something that is expensive both financially and emotionally, but you've got a recommendation from someone you know — it's the friend you know, like, and trust. That feeling of security is still in play.

So, what does that mean for you? We've already dealt with how your fave kinds of clients realise they need coaching services. But why would they buy from you?

Again, there's a whole bundle of reasons, not least because you're fabulous, right? Right! Just look at you sitting there in that top. MWAH! Chef's kiss!

But for people to buy coaching-type services from you they have to be aware of you, like what you're about, and trust that you'll be able to deliver what they want.

We have arrived at another kind of journey – the You Awareness journey.

The You Awareness journey

The You Awareness Journey maps the process someone (preferably an ideal client) goes through from not knowing a Scooby Doo about you, to not only being aware of you but trusting that you know your stuff and believing you're able to deliver on the things you say you help people with.

1. Unaware of you

V

2. Aware of you

V

3. Like you

V

4. Trust you

1. Unaware of you

They don't know you exist, and they can't buy from you if they don't know you exist!

2. Aware of you

Next, they become aware of you. But they might not know what you do yet or that what you do could help them.

3. Like you

Here, they start to get to know you a bit better. Maybe they've read a couple of your blog posts or heard you on a podcast. Either way, they've started to like what you're about. "This person is speaking my language," they think to themselves.

4. Trust you

Finally, it clicks into place — trust. "Yes, this coach is fab. They get me. I trust that they can help me."

But even as they get to this place of trust, it doesn't mean they'll start scouring your website or emails and hitting that "book a call" button.

Why not? It all comes together in the next chapter...

Chapter 3 Summary: What was that all about then?

Know, like, and trust is still alive and well and an essential part of the process a client will go through before making a decision.

Your turn

Answer the following questions to get a steer on how you're going with that know, like, trust factor:

- When you go to a conference or networking event

where some of your ideal clients go, how many people know who you are?

- When people book discovery calls with you, do you get a sense they've already seen you on social media, had a look at your website, or know quite a lot about how you work already? Or do they ask you picky questions about what you charge and how you work?
- How often do you use photos or videos of yourself in your social media posts and emails?
- If several of your biz besties were asked what kinds of people you're particularly skilled at helping and what you help them with, would they answer accurately?

Download the printable companion worksheets at:

janinecoombes.co.uk/yes-resources

Chapter 4
Getting to an easy yes

So many theoretical funnels and buyer journeys are unhelpful for coach-shaped-people because they muddle up whether the potential client is ready to take action with whether they're ready to work with *you*.

This is not how coaching clients function! They don't magically become aware of their desire to make a change in their life when you turn up in their world. And conversely, just because they're aware of what they "desire" to change doesn't mean they're sold on *you* being the person to help them with that change. Yes, it'd be lovely if that was how it worked but:

a. The world is a complex place.
b. People aren't that obedient.
c. It cuts out the people who are ready to buy *now* but who don't know you yet.

You can and should still try to reach these people.

I noticed this glitch in the matrix during a conversation with a client of mine. I'd been trying to help her plan her content so she was covering all the steps along the road for best-fit clients to work with her. I tried using one of the many linear models to plot it all out i.e. meeting potential clients where they were when they're only just finding out about their wants, all the way to decision making and action taking with the aim of helping them make the best purchasing decision for them.

But it's always a bit sticky. Because someone who's ready and able to buy now, doesn't necessarily know you exist. And someone who absolutely loves you down to your squishy guts, doesn't necessarily believe they've got a problem you're helping to solve. Or they don't realise you do the thing they want because you haven't made it clear...

And, thus, we come to the **Easy Yes** model.

Instead of having the Desire Awareness Journey all tangled up with the You Awareness journey, let's separate them and set them freeeee!

Let's present them on two axes:

Desire awareness journey

Decision time

Desire aware
solution aware

Desire aware
solution unaware

No desire for
change

Don't know
you   Aware   Like   Trust

You awareness journey

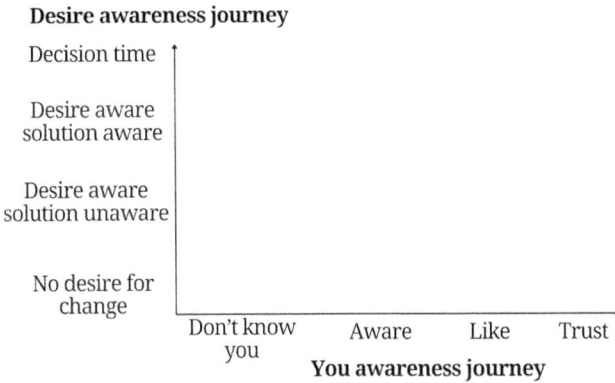

How the Easy Yes model works

It's fair to say that if someone resonates *hard* with everything you put out into the universe *and* they're ready to take action, they are highly likely to give you a massively Easy Yes. (As long as you offer them something that matches what they're looking for. More on that later).

I've marked the Easy Yes spot on the chart below. This is what we're aiming for with all our sales and marketing efforts — to arm people with all the info they need about us and whether what we do can help them achieve what they want.

Desire awareness journey

```
Decision time        ↑                              ┌────────┐
                     |                              │ EASY   │
Desire aware         |                              │ YES    │
solution aware       |                              └────────┘
                     |
Desire aware         |
solution unaware     |
                     |
No desire for        |
change               └─────────────────────────────────────────→
                       Don't know      Aware     Like      Trust
                       you
                            You awareness journey
```

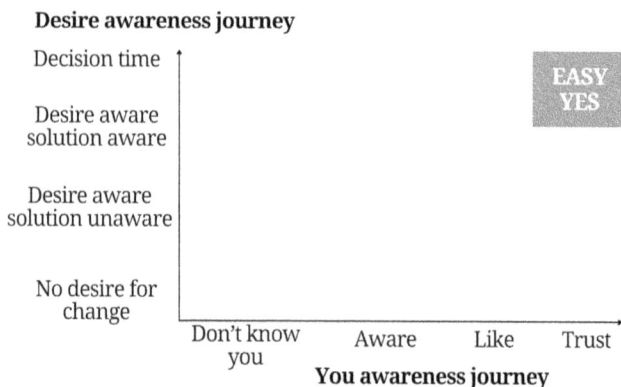

A personal example of this is when I was struggling through a period of bereavement and illness in the family. I already knew the power of coaching. I also knew I was struggling and couldn't cope on my own anymore. A friend recommended her coach who blended coaching with therapy and I was ready to pay before I'd even spoken to him! The Know Like Trust factor rested on the fact that I've known my friend for decades and I've seen with my own eyes how much he'd helped her, so I was a resounding "Easy Yes."

The power of word of mouth is still alive and kicking. But relying solely on referrals can be risky. I've had several extremely talented and experienced coaches come to me bamboozled as to why, after a couple of decades, their leads had suddenly dried up and they had no obvious way to get any more because they'd never done any marketing. If this is you, the Easy Yes framework will set you off in the right direction!

The Dead Zone

On the other hand, if you offer to help someone who doesn't believe they need what you're selling and doesn't know who you are from Adam, they're not going to buy. Why would they? That would be ridiculous!

This is why we hate cold direct messages so much. Some rando messaging us out of the blue telling us our website is rubbish and they could fix it for us? Jog on!

The Dead Zone is in the bottom left-hand of the chart. Let's get out of it ASAP!

Desire awareness journey

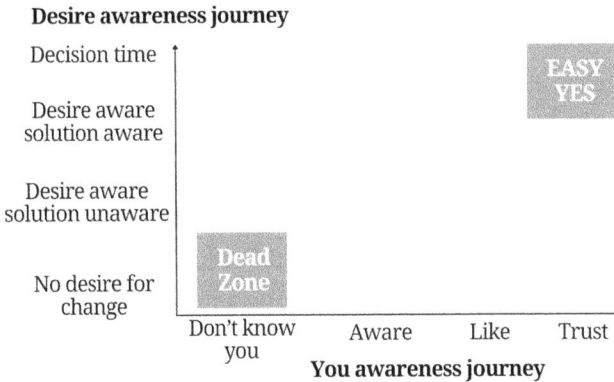

Chart showing "Desire awareness journey" on the vertical axis with levels: Decision time, Desire aware solution aware, Desire aware solution unaware, No desire for change. The horizontal axis "You awareness journey" shows: Don't know you, Aware, Like, Trust. A "Dead Zone" box is in the bottom left and an "EASY YES" box is in the top right.

The Easy Yes model lets spot why someone isn't buying when you know they'd be a perfect fit for your coaching. It also allows you to decide where to allocate your time when it comes to sales and marketing. For example, do enough people trust you can get the job done? If not, you probably need to work on nurturing your audience more and sharing more relevant testimonials.

In the next chapter, we're going to go into some examples so you can see how it all plays out.

Chapter 4 Summary: What was that all about then?

The Easy Yes sweet spot is when people who are ready to buy are the same people who know and trust you. As long as what you're offering appears relevant to them, they're going to buy.

Your turn

Think about a recent sales call that was successful where the client went on to buy from you. Did you get a sense that the person knew you already? Were they just on the call to clear up any final questions they had?

Think about a recent unsuccessful sales call when they said no. Were they absolutely clear on the situation they were in and what they needed to get the outcome they wanted? Or did you find yourself trying to convince them that what you did is what they needed?

Download the printable companion worksheets at:

janinecoombes.co.uk/yes-resources

Chapter 5
Using the Easy Yes model to get you more easy yeses

W e've touched on when an Easy Yes happens and what it looks like when you're dwelling in the Dead Zone. But there's a whole area in the middle where the model really comes to life.

If you've been blindsided by a perfect lead inexplicably saying no or beavering away at creating content for months and not getting any results from it, the Easy Yes model reveals what might really be going on below the surface.

How to make content marketing work for you

My ethos is that selling is not about convincing. You're not trying to bend someone's arm to get them to buy something that's not right for them. Instead, the aim is to help the client to make the best decision for them. Whether that's working with you or not.

And if you've already decided you're going to use content marketing in your coaching-shaped business, prospective clients are much more likely to work with you if you've used that content to guide them to their own Easy Yes. That said, this model still applies even if you don't create content or spend much time on social media. There are other ways of reaching people e.g. PR, networking, building a strategic referral network, and paid advertising.

If you meet people who are only just becoming aware of their desire for change, they're trying to work out what's going on. They will want to find out what solutions are available to them, which is when you can show up as their guide.

You can do this by creating helpful resources such as blog posts, podcasts, lead magnets or videos. Or even some sort of events like workshops or in-person networking. You can then be sure you've got content to help them at each step of the way. You'll be a trusted advisor. And they'll be left in no doubt that you know what they're going through and you're equipped to help.

Then, when they're in the position of being ready to part with some cash, you'll be the obvious choice.

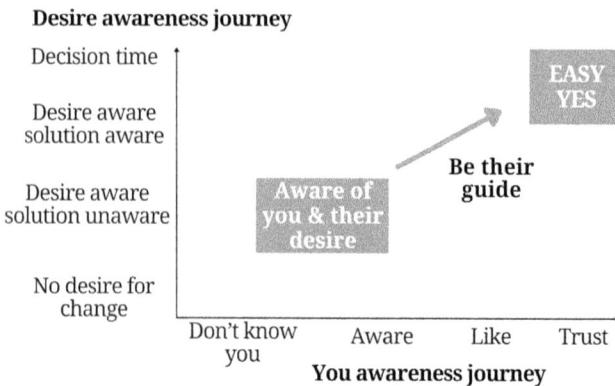

Desire awareness journey

Decision time

Desire aware
solution aware

Desire aware
solution unaware

No desire for
change

Don't know you · Aware · Like · Trust

Aware of you & their desire

Be their guide

EASY YES

You awareness journey

The joyful thing about this is that every message you craft and every piece of content you create can ooze you-ness. I stumbled upon the magic of this by accident back in 2018 when a friend of mine had her videos critiqued by a well-meaning viewer. He told her she needed to lower her voice, wear more make-up and, get this, "perhaps wear a set of pearls" to sound more credible!

Many were offended on her behalf, but it struck me as absolutely hysterical! I couldn't help myself. I slapped on as much make up as I could, put on my set of pearls I'd inherited from my gran, and videoed myself using a silly voice telling people how they should change themselves to be more credible. I was so nervous posting that video, but it was like I had been taken over and I had no choice.

The response was electric! Nobody was doing video on LinkedIn like that at the time. One woman even messaged me thanking me because she'd been going through a bout of prolonged ill health and depression and it was the first time she'd laughed in about a year. That kicked off my love of video marketing.

But you don't have to be wild and wacky to make an impact. You just have to be YOU. There are lots of people who show up fully as their calm selves. Using their own turn of phrase. Their own energy. And it lets people in and moves them along that Know like Trust journey.

At this point you might be thinking, "But I already create me-flavoured content regularly!" Yes, I hear you! You are not alone. There are so many people thrashing themselves trying to come up with daily social media posts, useful insights to send to their email subscribers, and rich long-form content like podcasts, videos and blogs. But have a look at the content you create for a moment...What stage of the Desire Awareness Journey is it for? I'm willing to bet it's probably clustered around one stage — desire-unaware. Amiright?

This is an absolute classic for coaches. They're so eager to help people they tend to focus on explaining how powerful their work is rather than talking about what their best fit clients actually *want*.

Truth bomb: People never buy "coaching." They're looking for some sort of outcome. That transformation is what they're paying for. They want to either move towards something they want to achieve, or move away from an unpleasant feeling or situation. Or both.

You absolutely can create materials for people who are desire-unaware, but for most coaches it shouldn't be a priority because these people are nowhere near buying yet. Better to focus on creating content for people who are searching for solutions and ready to take action. THEN you can build backwards and create guiding content for people who are earlier on in the Desire Awareness Journey.

What if not enough people are buying from you?

One of the things coaches struggle with is a simple lack of sales. Your content should be working to help you with this. For your ideal clients to reach an Easy Yes, your content should:

- Help them understand their situation e.g. "5 signs you'll burn out within 6 months"

- Show them what solutions are available to them e.g. "The careers guide for HR professionals and how to decide your next step."
- Cover decision-making topics e.g. "HRT vs Naturopath coach, which is best for you?"

If your marketing messages tick all those boxes and people are *still* not buying enough to make your coaching business thrive, it might be that not enough people know who you are. Awareness of you and what you do is especially key if you want to branch out from doing one-to-one coaching work. Once you get into the realms of one-to-many e.g. group programmes, retreats, memberships, and online courses, you're going to need to multiply your audience numbers many times over to be able to generate the leads you need to sell out those services.

What do I mean by audience? This could be your following on social media or people in your network. But all roads lead to your email list.

In an ideal world you'd be adding new people to your email list every week and gently letting them know how fabulous you are and how they can work with you on the regular.

The only three ways that you can get in front of new eyeballs:

1. Organically (aka grow your own)

By regularly producing content (blog posts, podcasts, video and online events) and sharing them far and wide, over time prospective clients will find you when they're searching online for topics you cover. People spreading the word about how fab you are fits into this category too. It's a slow burn, but it works.

2. Other people's audiences

A quicker way to boost the number of people who know you is to get in front of other people's audiences. Who do you know who serves a similar client type to you? Who has a podcast, video interview series, or runs summits to help these people? Find out if they'd feature you. N.B. This strategy works best if you have someone to direct them to. In other words, you've already ticked that organic "grow your own" audience box in some way.

3. Paid advertising

Last but not least, paid ads! You can pay to advertise on all the social media channels plus there's the option for Google ads. And no doubt many other options — paid ads is not my specialty. The coaches I know who are doing well with paid ads are driving traffic to some sort of freebie, then nurturing them on their email list before giving them an opportunity to engage with them more deeply e.g. a five-day challenge or webinar.

There are opportunities for them to say "yes" early on, but the point is the ads rarely promote high ticket coaching services directly. It's just not a great way to get good quality clients. Instead, the ultimate goal of all these activities is to encourage people to join your email list so you have permission to contact them in the future.

You *can* make sales directly from social media, selling from the stage, and through paid ads but it's difficult to crack! It feels easier and more pleasant, for you *and* the client, to foster trust with them and make offers via email or direct messaging once they've got to know you more. This goes back to the Easy Yes model — the more people know you and "get" what you do, the more likely they are to buy from you.

A note on networking

Whether it's in-person or online, a formal networking organisation or building friendships at conferences and other groups, networking can be a powerful way to build that *know like trust* factor with a group of people.

Networking can be a slow burn as it's tricky to land coaching clients having only met people once or twice! But the relationships you build usually pay back in many different ways over time. Not just in clients but in a trusted network, reducing feelings of loneliness and knowing the answer is "no" to the question: "Am I the only one who feels like this..?"

Still feeling like it's all a bit theoretical? Want some meaty examples? I hear ya. In the next chapter we'll dig into the Janine archives where I'll be sharing mini case studies of how the Easy Yes plays out in real life.

Chapter 5 Summary: What was that all about then?

Whether your favourite type of content to create is writing blogs, filming videos or recording podcasts, make sure you prioritise the last phase of the Desire Awareness Journey i.e. helping people to make a purchase decision.

There are only three ways to get in front of new people: organically, collaborating with other people in some way, and paid advertising. Pick the combination of channels and media that suit you and your personality.

Your turn

- What's your favourite way to create content? Are you playing to your strengths?
- Which audience-building strategy are you currently using?
- If someone who had a bustling community stuffed with your ideal clients asked you to share your wisdom with them, would you have an obvious place for them to go next? i.e. do you have a freebie to share with them?

Download the printable companion worksheets at:

janinecoombes.co.uk/yes-resources

Chapter 6
Troubleshooting
Why best-fit clients aren't doing what you want them to

Sometimes even when we've put everything into place and we think we're speaking to people at the Easy Yes sweet spot, things still go wonky. And it's so frustrating because if you don't know what went wrong, you can't fix it!

In this chapter, I'm going to run though the four "zones" of the Easy Yes model that most commonly ensnare coaches. This is when whipping out the Easy Yes model to do some troubleshooting will put the situation into perspective and help you work out what step you should take next. I guarantee that at least one of the examples I share will echo experiences you've had!

1. The Cool Referral Zone: Why didn't that hot lead buy?

Alex, a team performance expert and coach, came to me rather distraught. She'd been handed a peach of a referral from a friend. A blue-chip company wanting impostor syndrome training for their senior management team. This was absolutely the work she wanted more of!

She had prepared her pitch. Got her numbers together. Then presented her little socks off in the meeting. But the guy she was presenting to interrupted and asked for the price almost immediately. (This is often a red flag.) When she told him, he screwed his face up and said, "That's too much."

This was absolutely gutting for Alex. She'd gone in with a keen price and she wanted that contract so badly. But there was no way it could be done for any less.

The following week, I talked her through the Easy Yes model, and it became clear that the sticking point wasn't really the price at all. It was that they didn't really believe they had an issue with impostor syndrome in their company. They were desire-unaware. Or they genuinely didn't have a problem with impostor syndrome. Either way, they'd engaged her because they'd heard the buzz about impostor syndrome and were looking for a quick tick-in-box exercise. Alex's solution wasn't a five hundred quid lunch 'n' learn so the buyers were "out."

Once Alex could see this sale was never a goer, not only did she feel better, but she could start channelling her efforts to reach people who were more serious about making a purchase. And she was able to vet prospects more closely so she wouldn't waste time preparing pointless pitches in the future.

To add further context to this example, Alex was hitherto unknown to the client company. So all in all, this opportunity was sitting quite a long way from the Easy Yes spot.

Desire awareness journey

2. The "Who Are You?" Zone: Why did that ideal client buy from someone else?

Why do amazing clients go and buy from someone else even though you know you're the utterly best person to help them? This is such a frustrating situation to be in. I should know, I've been there!

You have someone who appears interested in working with you. They're making all the right noises. You hop on a call together. They ask for time to think about it. You even set up a follow up call to make a decision. You've done everything right! But then they cancel the follow up call and say they've gone with another coach.

I once had an ideal client decide to go with another marketing coach because that person had run a five-day challenge, which delivered more value than the free 15-minute one-to-one audit call I'd given her. There is no way the reason she chose to go with a different service provider was because I hadn't run a five-day challenge! It was because she had gotten to know and trust that person more than me. So, while the prospective client was right at the top of the Desire Awareness Journey, I was only at the "Aware" spot on the You Awareness Journey. I was dangerously close to the "Who Are You?" zone.

Desire awareness journey

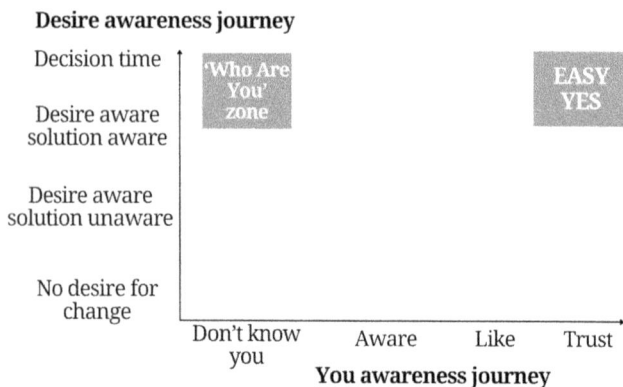

I regularly get clients who find themselves in this spot. They'd like more sales, and there are plenty of people out there who are ready to engage in coaching, but not enough of them know who they are. They haven't experienced that, "Ooh, this person is for *me*!" feeling.

I cover the three main ways you can help people get to know you in Chapter 5. As a reminder these are: organically, getting in front of other people's audiences and paid advertising. The key here is to keep at it and be patient. It takes time to get to know someone and for them to trust you with their inner thoughts.

3. The Fabulous (but Not-For-Me Zone): Why are buyer lead times so long?

When you're selling your services to corporate clients, it's taken as given that the lead times for a purchase to go through are on the long side. But can something be done to shorten them?

My client Kate, a leadership coach, was getting fed up with client companies taking eighteen months and more to decide to buy from her.

In some cases, it'd take her that long to get the first invoice signed, and then things would stall! Monetary resources had been committed to her services but not the headcount to set it all into motion. The project would just sit there for another six months, which was extremely frustrating for Kate who's itching to make a difference in the world.

I asked her to explain who she was aiming to work with and in what scenarios they'd need her help. And then I took her through the Easy Yes model. After a little probing, it turned out that most of Kate's sales and marketing efforts were aimed at people very early on in the Desire Awareness journey. She could see which people needed her, but those same people weren't really convinced they had a problem yet. So, despite them knowing and trusting her, they weren't taking any action for ages.

Kate's efforts had largely been dwelling at the bottom right of the chart. She'd been trying her hardest to explain to people she already had a relationship with that they needed to take action *now* — before their minor niggles became serious and more expensive to resolve.

Desire awareness journey

Decision time

Desire aware
solution aware

Desire aware
solution unaware

No desire for
change

				EASY YES
				Kate's sales efforts

Don't know
you   Aware   Like   Trust

You awareness journey

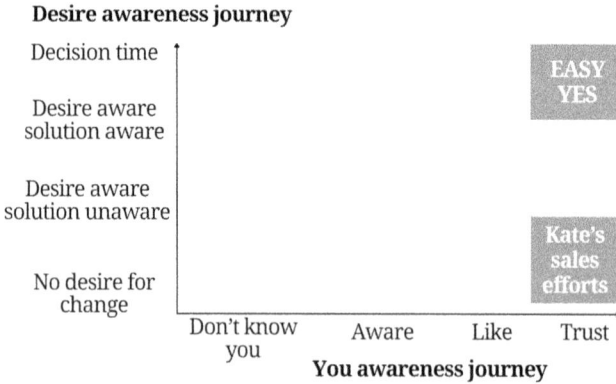

Kate had thought these long periods of trying to convince clients to nip their issues in the bud were a symptom of the corporate clients she was serving. But now she had an action plan, she could guide people through the process of understanding what they needed and she was able to update her sales materials accordingly. What this looked like was:

- Getting clear on what their exact symptoms were just prior to a company taking action so she could highlight them and start educating her audience.
- Do some research so she could describe what they were experiencing *in their own words.*
- Matching her offerings to what those client companies *were* ready to buy rather than trying to sell them the full solution of what she knew they needed. (But that they didn't *think* they needed yet.)

Now Kate was able to identify what it looked like when her ideal client companies were *already aware* they needed to take action, what kinds of solutions they'd be looking into, and what those trigger points were. That meant she could spot when people were ready to buy instead of trying to convince people they needed her when they didn't even realise they had a problem yet.

This is a common stumbling block that catches most people sooner or later — even seasoned marketers. We *so* want to help people before their situation gets too dire that we waste a lot of breath trying to sell people *what we know they need*. If this doesn't match what's in the prospective client's head, they simply won't be able to see it's for them no matter how persuasive you are with your arguments.

Instead, you need to sell them what they WANT. You can still give them what they NEED. For example, someone might be having a nightmare with their direct reports. What they NEED is better leadership skills but what they WANT is for their team to stop complaining and get on with their jobs without having to be micromanaged all the time. In this case, if you position your services as a "team turnaround" service as opposed to leadership training, you're more likely to get some takers.

4. The Friend Zone: Why do people who vibe with your message not buy?

This is a sticking point that crops up regularly with my clients! Especially those who're working with individuals who haven't had personal coaching before. When people see their website and social media posts they love them! They ask if they're mind readers. They say, "Yes! I was just saying this to my friend the other day!" And then don't take any action.

Persuading people that they need coaching is exhausting, feels unethical, and rarely works. But staying in the Friend Zone isn't an option if you want a thriving coaching business.

Desire awareness journey

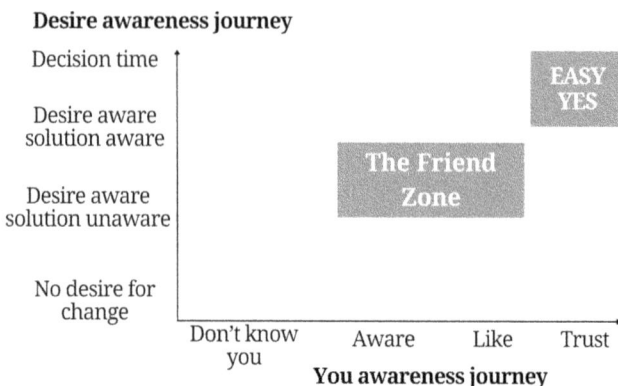

If you're in this situation there could be a couple of different things at play:

1. You're not known by enough of the right people yet. In other words, you have an audience volume issue. Have a look back at Chapter 5 on the three ways to resolve that.
2. You don't cater your messaging or calls to action to people who are at that awkward "want to take action, can't take action" stage.

I've also seen people shy away from being too on the nose with calling out their prospective clients' struggles. It feels like you're poking your finger in their bruise. Horrible! I've heard people call it "pain point marketing" which makes that bruise-poking guilt even more pronounced.

How about calling it empathy marketing instead? The coaches who are getting fully booked are meeting their prospective clients where they are. They don't shy away from calling out in their messaging how their potential clients are feeling and what they want instead. If people don't realise you can help them, they'll either dribble along in the same state until something drastic happens. Or they'll work with another coach who may or may not be as committed and honest as you.

This stage is simultaneously the most fun for me to work on with clients and the most challenging because it means slowing everything down. We dig into the potential client's psyche with compassion and empathy, which requires patience. You'll probably feel like yelling, "Why the hell aren't you buying? Can't you see I can help you? Gah!"

For argument's sake, let's imagine a situation where the prospective client in question:

- Knows you and believes you're amazing at what you do.
- They're very aware of their current, uncomfortable situation and what they want instead.
- And they're aware that coaching exists as a solution.

But there's a block in the way. A barrier between what they want and you. One of my clients, Lisa, is a wellness coach for people pleasers and was in exactly this situation. She'd get raving fans replying to her emails and her social media posts and they'd always attend her free webinars, but few people were buying. So we sat down together, went through the Easy

Yes model and worked out what on earth we could do with these Friend Zone prospects.

Lisa's clients were absolutely wrung out. They were so used to putting other people first it seemed alien to suddenly splash the cash on coaching *for themselves*. Not to mention time and space dedicated to working on how they'd like their life to be different. How self-indulgent! What sort of person would do such a thing? Not them, that's for sure!

And yet how can they get themselves out of this self-destructive spiral they're in without external help? Liz's clients need some or all of the following:

- **Permission** to focus on themselves e.g. explaining that by doing this work they're helping others in their life.
- **Proof** that people like them do things like this e.g. showing them that other people in their situation have worked with you and made the changes they're seeking.
- **Reassurance** that your methods will work *for them* and that they are capable of doing the work needed e.g. sharing testimonials from people like them who have experienced the kind of transformation they're looking for.
- **Match** what you're saying to what they really want. Not what you *think* they want. And not even what they *say* they want. But deep down what's driving them. You can get to this by conducting in-depth research interviews with a selection of ideal clients. Another way to do this is gather up your notes of what people said just as they start to work with you

and when they start to see a shift in their being. What opportunities and differences does your work ultimately unlock for them? How do they describe this?

The way Liz transmitted all this detail was to weave it through her marketing materials including her emails, social media posts, and presentations.

So, now you've got a bunch of people who think the sun shines out of your derrière, and they're firmly in the position of making a purchasing decision. They'll deffo buy now, right?

Not so fast!

There's one more hurdle to leap over. One that many people think they've nailed, but they haven't...

———

Chapter 6 Summary: What was that all about then?

If you have a referral who looks tip top but they inexplicably say no, you could be in the "Cool Referral Zone."

If you have people who appear to know, like and trust you, but they're still not buying, you could be in the "Fabulous (but not for me) Zone."

If you're having conversations with people who look like an absolutely perfect fit for your services, but they're trotting off and working with other coaches, you could be dwelling in the "Who are you?" Zone.

And if you're churning out high quality content your ideal customer seems to love but they're still not buying, you could be stuck in the Friend Zone.

The solution to all four scenarios is to be aware of where they're sitting on the framework and then prioritise actions to move your audience more towards the Easy Yes spot.

Your turn

- Look at your last five instances of people turning down the opportunity to work with you and categorise them.
- Which area(s) do you need to prioritise in your marketing?

For more support with this, go to the book resources vault at:

janinecoombes.co.uk/yes-resources

Chapter 7
The easy no (and how to avoid it)

Allow me now to introduce you to Clarence. He's the elephant in the room. There he is, standing in a corner. Big and lumbering. I see you, Clarence!

He's here to tell you there's a piece of the puzzle we haven't covered yet. But first, let's have a quick recap…

We've got you to the point that your favourite types of clients know you're the bee's knees and trust you can help them move towards what they want. They're in a place where they not only understand their situation and how they want their world to be different, but they're also aware of all the options open to them and they've decided to go with some sort of coach.

One thing stands in the way of you and the easiest sale you have ever made: your offer.

A few years ago, I did a sales course. It went heavy on the accountability and very light on the clarification of what you were actually selling. I could immediately tell who was going to do well in the programme. And who wasn't. Some people were offering services that people obviously would want. And some people's offers made no sense at all.

Lo and behold, me and my crystal ball were right! I remember a group call where one woman was selling something so obviously nonsense and explaining to the trainer that it just wasn't shifting. The trainer's response? More posting, more emailing, more DMs. MORE!

This experience underlined what I've learned in my years of education, my career in big corporates, and working with coach-shaped-people. How you position what you do has to be as clear and crisp as one of those winter days when the sun's shining but your nose feels like it's about to drip icicles.

If you can't concisely articulate what you're selling and why your best-fit clients should buy it, how on earth will they know that you hold the answer to their dreams?

The subject of how to craft an Easy Yes *Offer* deserves its own book. But I'll give you an overview here, so you're not left dangling.

The 3 Ps of an Easy Yes Offer

Your offer is absolutely key. It has the power to position you as a must-have in the eyes of ready-to-buy best fit clients. It's also an exercise in clarity.

Going through my Easy Yes Offer process forces you to get precise on who you're serving, how you help and why they should pick you over other coaches. From my years of working on offers, messaging, and helping coaches, I've noticed there are three sections to an offer that is easy to sell.

1. The Promise

No, you won't literally say to a client "I promise you this result." We'd have a revolt in the legal profession if we did that! I call it the Promise because it's what you'd love to be able to promise your best fit clients.

What are the results you can achieve when a perfect client shows up and goes all in? How did they feel before working with you? How is their life afterwards? What kind of transformation have they experienced?

We're not talking about how you describe the entirety of what you do here. We're talking offer-level messaging. What you'd put on a sales page not what you'd put on your homepage. When you get it right, the reader will get an emotional reaction. A feeling that shouts, "omg has this person bugged my house?!" That's what we're looking for here. It's what will call your best-fit clients to you and show them it's *you* they need to work with. Specifically, through this offer you've just shared with them.

Here's an example of the sort of copy I see a lot of:

> "Being a good leader is essential for high productivity and lower staff turnover, saving money, and creating a better work environment for your employees. Ask me about my leadership coaching services."

This is selling what people *need* and not putting it in terms of what they *want*. Here's an example of how you could flip that:

> "Are you a senior HR professional who's been given a challenging target for better staff retention this year? Somehow you need to deliver this while staying within budget and increasing productivity. The Competitive Edge programme is designed for board level personnel and targets the five key areas of successful leadership. Also, it can be billed through your training budget."

This is an entirely fictional piece of messaging, but hopefully you can see I've imagined that the ideal customer in this scenario is probably an HR director who's under pressure and feeling squeezed in a business where being a market leader is the order of the day and budgets are tight.

2. The Package

Whereas the Promise makes a strong emotional "click" that shows your ideal clients your offer is the right fit for them, the Package backs up that heartfelt decision with the rational ticks in boxes.

The Package on its own won't sell what you do. It needs to be in a format that shows your ideal clients what your work consists of. It needs to answer questions like:

- How does this all work?
- Will this actually work for *me*?
- Will they make me do anything weird that I'll hate?

So, whether you have a step-by-step process that you take clients through, or whether you simply hold space for your clients and guide them to their own decisions, there's a way to represent that in a clear, compelling way. You might have seen coaches with their own "signature system." This is where that sits — in the Package.

The three main reasons to get your Package right:

1. So it makes sense for the price you're charging.
2. To remove any questions and doubts about how you achieve the results you do.
3. To make sure those heads that started nodding with the emotional messaging *keep* nodding.

On a typical sales page you'd connect with people using emotional reasoning (Promise) then consolidate using the Package. So instead of:

"You can buy a package of 6 coaching calls, 12 coaching calls or 18 coaching calls. Includes values audit, personality tests, and quarterly group calls."

You'd have something like:

"The Competitive Edge leadership programme is based on my 5-part VIPER model:

V: Values and vision alignment — 90 min facilitated workshop

I: Individual strengths assessment for all participants

P: Planning and goal setting

E: Edge coaching calls — conducted one-to-one online, fortnightly

R: Reflection and relational progress sessions — quarterly group calibration"

I realise this probably sounds a bit cheesy and not based in reality – that's because I just made it up! But you can see how much more robust and valuable the second iteration sounds. It won't win the work on its own as it needs to follow a promise that's already got the right people champing at the bit because it sounds so much like what they need right now.

Once a client has seen that you "get" them, and you have a sensible roadmap to get them where they want to go, *then* you state the price.

3. The Price

Ahh, don't we all just love pricing up our services! No? Just me then...

Pricing is both less important and more important than you might think. It is *less important* because people don't make decisions on whether they want to buy something based on the price. Not high-quality coaching-type services anyway. They might see the price and then decide they can't afford it, granted. But if the Promise properly resonates with them, the Package makes total sense, and they're in that golden Easy Yes spot, they will be way more likely to try and get the funds together to pay whatever price you've put on it.

Let me make this crystal clear: people don't buy high-touch coaching services because they're cheap.

This is not something people take a punt on. This is a considered life decision or a major business investment. Not just because of the price but because of the time they'll be spending with you. And the potentially deeply private information you'll be privy to.

And pricing is *more important* than you might think because I've seen too many coaches discount their work thinking it's going to be easier to sell (which doesn't work) and then they have to sell even more spots and service many more clients to make the same amount of money. Driving them into the ground with overwork. That makes me so sad.

Maths time! If you offer coaching at £100 for two monthly sessions, then you'd need 50 clients to reach a modest £5k revenue per month. Fifty! I need a nap just thinking about that. But if you sold your main coaching package at £500 per month, you'd need ten clients. Much more manageable both from a sales point of view and from a client delivery standpoint.

Does the thought of quintupling your prices make you sick up in your mouth a bit? Yes, arbitrarily whacking your prices up does feel crap when it's not rooted in a true representation of the value you bring. Which is why I always deal with Pricing as the last P when I work with clients.

Once you're clear on the full value of what you help people with, you'll be able to price from a place of pride. You'll know you're delivering good value even at a higher-level price. And you'll feel confident that your clients are getting a good deal. You'll be able to feel it's a proper win-win.

If you've taken a look at where a potential client is on the Easy Yes model and they appear to be in the Easy Yes spot, but they're still hesitating — the Easy Yes Offer is often the final bit of the puzzle.

Chapter 7 Summary: What was that all about then?

You may have people who are absolutely ready to buy some sort of coaching *and* they know you're wonderful, but if your offer is presented in a wishy-washy way they still might not buy.

There are three elements to a compelling Easy Yes Offer: the Promise, the Package, and the Price.

Your turn

Think of the service you love to deliver most. And the one that's the easiest to sell and gets the best results for your clients. Now answer these questions:

Promise

- If you had an amazing potential client sat in front of you right now, would you be able to explain concisely why your service is for them?

Package

- Do you run clients through a step-by-step process or

a set of pillars, principles, or methodologies that you draw on?

- Is there any aspect of the way you work that's unusual or needs explanation?

Price

- What price do you currently charge for this service?
- Picture a client saying yes to your offer at this price then tune into how you feel about delivering all that work at that level. Does it make you feel excited or do you have a sinking almost resentful pull in your gut?

Go to janinecoombes.co.uk/yes-resources for more support on crafting an easy yes offer.

Putting it all into action

Hopefully you've now got a much better handle on what your sales and marketing activities are doing for your business and where your audience is sitting on the Easy Yes model as a whole — and also how to diagnose sales problems when they arise.

I came up with the Easy Yes model to make marketing simpler for my clients. To help them spot why some things aren't working and where to focus their attention in future.

As a coach-shaped-person, you're unlikely to need more stuff to do. More tactics to master. More marketing channels to manage. More information to digest. More more more is usually a one way ticket to overwhelm, not clarity and progress! But now you have a way to see what you've got already and what it's doing for you, putting the reins back in your hands.

I certainly needed this perspective shift when I first started my business; from scurrying along the ground to standing back and seeing my marketing as a whole. All those wasted hours trying to find the hack that was going to magically unlock success in my business.

There are no hacks. There's only you, your skills and how, where, and when you present what you can do for people.

The next time you have the opportunity to get in front of people who you know would absolutely shine because of working with you, it'll be more straightforward for you to know what you need to do next.

I'm going to wrap up with a few questions that are likely to arise having finished reading this book. If you read through these and still have ponderings to share, I'd love to hear from you. Head on over to the resource vault at janinecoombes.co.uk/yes-resources and send 'em to me.

Q1. When could I use the Easy Yes model?

Use it when someone has expressed an interest in working with you. Whip it out when you've been handed a lead, or if someone's booked in for a sales call with you. It'll prompt you to do some digging to find out where they are on the Desire Awareness Journey and how well they know you. How could you find this out? You could DM them and ask some questions! If you use a calendar booking app, you could include a few questions they need to answer before picking a spot in your diary.

You can also use the Easy Yes model when you're planning out your marketing content. Whether it's a blog, podcast, video series, or just your next few months' social media posts that you're plotting out, have a look at which area of the Easy Yes model you want to focus on. Have you created enough content helping people who are looking to buy now-ish? Or have you done enough of that but you have a gap helping people understand their problems and desires more?

Q2. What can I expect to happen when I put the Easy Yes model into practice?

In a word, clarity. When a keen client decides not to work with you after all, you'll be able to work out what's going on. The likelihood is that either they weren't ready to take action yet, they don't trust that you're the person to help enough yet, or your offer didn't resonate enough with them. Those insights can be painful when you really want to work with that person! But now you know what you need to do next to reduce the likelihood of that happening again.

So the second benefit of putting the Easy Yes model into action is you'll be able to plan your marketing efforts more efficiently. You'll know where to focus your efforts. You'll know what topics you need to cover to make sure you're guiding people to the best decision for them. And you'll be able to notice when your coaching offer needs refining.

Q3. How can I take action on this without getting myself overwhelmed?

Take it one step at a time. Have you got a sales call booked in your diary? Can you find that person on social media? Have you spoken to them before? Do some detective work and see if you can tell where that person is sitting on the Easy Yes model. Is there anything you could ask them before the call that'll help you understand their interpretation of their desire for change? This greater understanding of where they're coming from is at the heart of every worthwhile and ethical sales conversation.

Want more Easy Yeses in your life?

Now you can use the Easy Yes model to help you fill in the blanks in the most you-flavoured way possible and start seeing real traction towards a truly thriving and joyful coaching business. Hurrah!

Naturally, it's harder when you're trying to do it yourself out in the wild. If you've spotted some areas you want to work on with a marketing professional like me, here are some options:

- Download the Easy Yes resources at janinecoombes.co.uk/yes-resources
- Connect with me on LinkedIn: linkedin.com/in/janinecoombes
- Check out my website and fantastic content (even if I do say so myself) at: janinecoombes.co.uk

I would really appreciate a review on Amazon! And feel free to buy extra copies to generously give to your coachy friends.

Acknowledgments

Starting with the obvious one — thanks to Vicky Quinn Fraser who coached me through the process of writing this small but (hopefully) impactful book, and for the beautiful typesetting and proofreading. There was zero chance I was going to get it all done on my own!

And Amy Warren, who swooped in like a knight in shining armour (can armoured people swoop..?) and helped me get this book over the line. Editing and detail work is NOT my forté. The book is ten times better than it would've been without her expert eye.

My gratitude also goes to Clare Josa who was the person who originally got me to believe I had a book in me and who has spent so much of her precious time with me in the past years, sharing advice, coaching me through half my first book which I decided not to publish but which helped me steer my business to calmer waters.

Fruit baskets and homemade noodle soup of appreciation to my illustrator, book cover designer, and oldest serving friend Rebecca Capper (that's Reb to you, but Bec to me). How wonderful that after 35 years of friendship I can wedge a massive piece of work like this into her schedule with pretty much no notice. That's what friends are for!

Lashings of thanks to my amazing and generous BETA readers too! I don't really know what I was expecting from you but it wasn't the depths of seriousness and care you took the task to. The result is magnitudes better than it would have been without your input. And so, in order of how you were on my excel spreadsheet: Meg Lyons, Kate Davis, Lucy Davies, Naomi Withers, Louise Miller, Teresa Heath-Wareing, Gudrun Lauret, Fiona Brennan, Rachel Extance, Kaye King, Mike Garner, Jacqui Jagger, and Clare Josa, you all have a massive favour awaiting you. Give me a bell whenever you choose to redeem it!

Deep and heartfelt credit to all my coaches who've all helped me piece together who I really am through the years. You have helped me "find out who I am and do it on purpose" more and more with every day: Vinty Firth, Jessica Fearnley, Jacqui Jagger, Louise Miller, Kate Davis, and Nick Harris.

A resounding shout out to the amazing Lyndsay Cambridge and Martin Huntbach of Jammy. Pretty much everything I learned about content marketing, I absorbed from them. My work has been influenced and vastly improved by their feedback from when I was in their membership, and their book *Content Fortress*. Which is *excellent*. I hope this book is even half as good as theirs.

I should probably also thank my kids, Austin and Josie. In all honesty they didn't help me to write this book. They probably impeded my progress if anything. But I do love them! Sincere thanks to Rich, my husband, though. Your pep talks are unparalleled! And I wouldn't have even dreamt of writing a book without your support.

Oh and my mum, dad, and sister! (This is turning into an Oscar acceptance speech...) From the moment I mentioned that I might write a book they encouraged me, despite not really understanding what I do for a living.

And HUGE thanks to you, you gorgeous human! I appreciate you buying this book. Spending your hard-earned money and precious time here. What would be the point of this book without you reading it?

I really hope I've managed to spark a few extra ideas or put some things into context so you can move your coaching-shaped business forwards in a purposeful and 100% you-flavoured way.

About the Author

Janine Coombes is a marketing consultant who helps coach-shaped-people earn more without slogging their guts out with marketing that doesn't work. She's particularly skilled at making it easier to attract more of your favourite kinds of clients by clarifying your messaging and the positioning of your coaching offers.

She has an extensive background in business and marketing including working with big brands like EE, Orange, and Europcar. Janine has a business degree, a post-graduate marketing diploma (CIM Dip), and she's spoken at some of the biggest entrepreneur events such as Atomicon, You Are The Media and MarketEd.Live.

www.ingramcontent.com/pod-product-compliance
Ingram Content Group UK Ltd.
Pitfield, Milton Keynes, MK11 3LW, UK
UKHW022216280525
6129UKWH00004B/295

9 781068 582707